CW00832654

About this Learning Guide

Shmoop Will Make You a Better Lover*
*of Literature, History, Poetry, Life...

Our lively learning guides are written by experts and educators who want to show your brain a good time. Shmoop writers come primarily from Ph.D. programs at top universities, including Stanford, Harvard, and UC Berkeley.

Want more Shmoop? We cover literature, poetry, bestsellers, music, US history, civics, biographies (and the list keeps growing). Drop by our website to see the latest.

www.shmoop.com

Table of Contents

Introduction 3
   In a Nutshell 3
   Why Should I Care? 3
Summary 4
   Book Summary 4
   Section I (Muriel in the Hotel) 4
   Section II (Seymour on the Beach and in the Hotel) 5
Themes 7
   Theme of Innocence 7
   Questions About Innocence 7
   Chew on Innocence 7
   Theme of Madness 7
   Questions About Madness 7
   Chew on Madness 8
   Theme of Spirituality 8
   Questions About Spirituality 8
   Chew on Spirituality 8
   Theme of Isolation 8
   Questions About Isolation 8
   Chew on Isolation 8
   Theme of Sex 8
   Questions About Sex 9
   Chew on Sex 9
Quotes 9
   Innocence Quotes 9
   Madness Quotes 11
   Spirituality Quotes 14
   Isolation Quotes 15
   Sex Quotes 16
Plot Analysis 17
   Classic Plot Analysis 17
Study Questions 19
Characters 19
   All Characters 19
      Seymour Glass Character Analysis 19
      Seymour Glass Timeline and Summary 21
      Sybil Carpenter Character Analysis 21
      Sybil Carpenter Timeline and Summary 23
      Muriel Glass Character Analysis 23
      Muriel Glass Timeline and Summary 24
   Character Roles 25
   Character Clues 25
Literary Devices 26

Symbols, Imagery, Allegory 26
Setting 27
Narrator Point of View 27
Genre 28
Tone 28
Writing Style 28
What's Up with the Title? 29
What's Up with the Epigraph? 29
What's Up with the Ending? 30
Did You Know? 31
Trivia 31
Steaminess Rating 32
Allusions and Cultural References 32
Best of the Web 32
Videos 32
Audios 33
Images 33
Documents 33
Websites 33

Introduction

In a Nutshell

American author J.D. Salinger is most famous for his novel _Catcher in the Rye_, published in 1951. But before the infamous Holden Caulfield came the Glass family – the focus of many of Salinger's most well-known short stories.

The Glass family is a fictional creation of Salinger, featuring seven children of staggering intelligence, wisdom, and precociousness. These characters pop up again and again in Salinger's short stories, either as the main characters or as peripheral connections. And it all starts with "A Perfect Day for Bananafish," the story of Seymour Glass, the oldest of the Glass children.

Salinger wrote "Bananafish" in 1948 when he was still relatively unknown. In the story, Seymour Glass, just back from his service in World War II, struggles with mental illness while vacationing with his wife in Florida. The story explores themes of innocence, youth, and spirituality (a reflection of Salinger's growing interest in Zen Buddhism). The folks at _New Yorker_ were so impressed with the story that they published it immediately and signed a "right of first refusal" for any more of Salinger's stories. Thus Salinger was launched to fame – long before _Catcher in the Rye_.

"Bananafish" is famous not only as the beginning of the Glass family saga, but also for its highly enigmatic ending. We won't spoil it for you by giving anything away here, but the story's shocking and perhaps confusing conclusion has left critics debating Salinger's intentions, not to mention the real meaning of the story. Now that we've thoroughly enticed you, you can get to reading the story already.

Why Should I Care?

Clothes, cars, video games, food, TV – it's easy to like this stuff. It's easy to get caught up in material pleasures, to worry about what you're going to wear or what you look like or what's going to feel good. In fact, it's _normal_ to worry about this stuff. If you met someone who didn't give a hoot about any of it, you'd might think he or she was crazy.

"A Perfect Day for Bananafish" does two important things. One, it reminds us that there is more to life than clothes, food, and TV. Number two, it calls into question our definitions of words like "sane" and "crazy." (Or, in the words of a cheesy 90s action movie, "What if I told you insane was working fifty hours a week in some office?") When you shift around your perspective a little bit, when you start asking what's really important in life, you start to wonder if maybe we've got it all wrong, and the people we think of as "crazy" have got it right after all.

At least, that's the question Salinger inspires us to ask. Throw in some of the greatest dialogue written in the last fifty years and an adorable four-year-old girl, and you've got a short story that is definitely worth the fifteen minutes it will take you to read. And the fifteen years it will take you

to figure it out.

Summary

Book Summary

"A Perfect Day for Bananafish" takes place at a resort hotel in Florida in 1948. The first scene features Muriel Glass, a young woman who has been married for five years to Seymour Glass. Muriel is on the phone with her mother, discussing Seymour. It seems that, since getting back from the war (WWII), Seymour just hasn't been the same. He's mentally unstable, and seemingly incapable of functioning normally in a social environment. Muriel's mother is scared for her daughter and wants her to come home. But Muriel doesn't seem to be taking the issue very seriously at all. She insists that Seymour is fine.

The second scene takes place on the beach outside the hotel, where a little girl named Sybil Carpenter waits while her mother puts sun block on her back. "See more glass," the girl keeps repeating, though her mother has no idea what that means. Finally Mrs. Carpenter lets the little girl run off to play. Sybil runs to a deserted part of the beach to find Seymour, with whom she's apparently struck up a friendship during her stay at the hotel. Seymour is obviously wonderful with children; he jokes around with Sybil, and she's clearly enamored with him.

The two of them head into the ocean together, and Seymour explains to Sybil all about bananafish. They're normal little fish, he says, until they swim into a banana hole and gorge themselves on bananas. Then they're too fat to get back out again and they die. Sybil, playing along, exclaims that she's seen a bananafish with six bananas in its mouth. Seymour then kisses her foot and says it's time to go back.

Once they've parted ways, Seymour plods along back to the hotel. In the elevator, he accuses an adult woman of looking at his feet. She thinks he's crazy. Seymour makes it to his hotel room, where Muriel is asleep on one of the twin beds. He takes a gun from his suitcase, sits on the other bed, and fires a bullet through his temple.

Section I (Muriel in the Hotel)

- At a hotel filled with New York advertising men, a young woman in room 507 has to wait over two hours to get a phone call through. (This is the 1940s.) While she waits, she reads a magazine article called "Sex is Fun—or Hell," and takes care of some trivial matters (like painting her nails).
- When the phone finally rings, she waits to finish painting her nails before picking it up: "She looked as if her phone had been ringing continually since she reached puberty" (1.2).
- Finally, the operator puts her through to her mother, whom she had been trying to reach. We find out that the girl's name is Muriel, and that her mother is of the over-protective, domineering type.
- The conversation reveals that Muriel has just arrived in Florida for a vacation with her husband Seymour. It becomes clear that Seymour is not well, mentally, and that Muriel's

mother disapproves of him.

- She asks if Seymour tried any of that funny business with the trees while he drove; Muriel assures her that he drove just fine, and asks if Daddy fixed the car.
- Laughing, Muriel reveals that Seymour has a nickname for her: "Miss Spiritual Tramp of 1948."
- Muriel asks if she left a book of German poetry behind, given to her by Seymour. She explains that Seymour called this particular writer "the only great poet of our century" and told her she should learn German to read him (1.42).
- Muriel's mother goes back to actively disapproving of Seymour. She says that Muriel's father talked to Dr. Sivetski (probably a psychiatrist) about all the strange things Seymour has done lately (like that business with the trees, that business with the window, the horrible things he said to Muriel's grandmother about dying, etc.).
- And Dr. Sivetski thinks that Seymour was released too soon from the Army hospital (where we gather he was being treated for mental problems). They all fear he may lose control of himself completely.
- Muriel responds cavalierly. There is a therapist at the hotel, she says. She can't remember his name or anything, but he's "supposed to be very good" (1.56). She's clearly not as worried about Seymour as is her mother, and she starts complaining about the terrible sunburn she's gotten.
- Her mother brings the conversation back to the therapist at the hotel. Muriel gabs about his wife, whom she saw last night wearing an unflattering dress. She (the therapist's wife) kept asking if Seymour was related to Suzanne Glass.
- The small talk continues. The two women discuss fashion and the hotel in which Muriel and Seymour are staying.
- Muriel's mother keeps asking her if she's all right, if she wants to come home, if she feels unsafe, and if she wants to stay alone for a while instead of with Seymour. Muriel insists that she's fine. Her mother laments that Muriel waited for Seymour all through the war so faithfully.
- Muriel tries to end the conversation; Seymour might come in from the beach any minute, she says. Her mother worries that he's out there on the beach unsupervised, and she hopes that he will behave himself.
- Muriel says he's fine; he won't even take his bathrobe off – because he doesn't want people to see his tattoo, his says. Muriel then admits that he has no tattoo.
- After promising to call if anything goes wrong, Muriel finally gets off the phone.

Section II (Seymour on the Beach and in the Hotel)

Cut to the beach. A little girl named Sybil Carpenter sits on a beach ball while her mother spreads sun-tan oil on her shoulders. "See more glass," says Sybil, over and over. "Did you see more glass?" (2.1).
Sybil's mother finds this irritating, and sends her daughter off to play so she herself can go have a martini.
Left to her own devices, Sybil walks a quarter of a mile down the beach, away from the immediate bounds of the hotel. She stops where a young man is lying on his back. "Are you going in the water, see more glass?" she asks (2.10). ("See more glass" = "Seymour Glass")
Seymour opens an eye and greets Sybil by name. It seems they've made friends while staying

at the hotel.

Sybil tells Seymour that her father is coming tomorrow "on a nairplane" (2.17) and asks where "the lady" is (Muriel, we imagine). They lady, says Seymour, is inside the hotel room, having her hair dyed or making dolls for poor children.

Seymour compliments Sybil's blue bathing suit; she immediately reminds him, "this is a *yellow*" (2.21). Of course, says Seymour.

He chats playfully with the little girl, asking her what's new or what sign she is. Sybil, being a little girl, changes the subject. She accuses Seymour of letting Sharon Lipschutz sit on the piano bench with him.

Seymour admits that this is the case, but explains that there was nothing he could do about it when she came and sat down next to him. But, he says, he pretended she was Sybil.

Next time, push her off, says Sybil.

Seymour proposes that they go in the water and try to catch a bananafish. He stands up and takes off his robe. He is pale and wearing blue swim trunks. He then picks up his ill-inflated raft and heads for the water with Sybil.

Sybil says she's never seen a bananafish.

Seymour changes the subject; he asks where she lives. Sybil, walking "stomach foremost" (2.48) into the water, tells him (Whirly Wood, Connecticut) and asks if he has read *Little Black Sambo*.

Yes, says Seymour, he read it last night. He was amazed with how many tigers were in the story.

There were only six, says Sybil. Then she ask if Seymour likes wax (he does) and olives (yep) and Sharon Lipschutz.

What he likes about Sharon, says Seymour, is that she's never mean to the dogs in the lobby, whereas *some* little girls he knows like to poke the little dogs with sticks.

"I like to chew candles," responds Sybil. "Who doesn't?" says Seymour (2.2.66-7).

They finally go into the water; Seymour picks up Sybil and places her on the raft. He tells her to keep an eye out for bananafish, as this is a perfect day for bananafish.

Then he explains how bananafish work. They're ordinary-looking, he says, until they swim into a banana hole and gorge themselves on bananas. Then they're so fat they can't get out the hole again. And then…they die. They get banana fever, which is a terrible disease.

Seymour lets Sybil get doused by a wave that comes along; she's loving it. Then she reports that she's seen a bananafish – with six bananas in its mouth.

Seymour picks up one of Sybil's wet feet and kisses it on the arch. Then he tells her that they're going in to shore, though she protests.

Back on the sand, Sybil says goodbye and runs back towards the hotel. Seymour puts on his robe and cinches it up, before plodding back to the hotel himself.

In the hotel, Seymour gets into an elevator with an operator and a woman with zinc salve on her nose. "I see you're looking at my feet," he says to her, once the car starts moving (2.102).

The women explains that she was looking at the floor.

"Don't be a god-damned sneak about it," says Seymour. He then insists that he has normal feet and there's no reason why anybody should be staring at them (2.104).

Once he gets to his floor, he walks down to room 507. The room smells like nail polish. Muriel is asleep on one of the twin beds. Seymour goes over to his luggage, takes out an Ortgies caliber 7.65 automatic, sits down on the empty bed, looks at Muriel, and fires a bullet through his right temple.

Themes

Theme of Innocence

"A Perfect Day for Bananafish" contrasts the world of children (imaginative, curious, pure, and innocent) with the world of adults (materialistic, selfish, shallow). As you can see, the story glorifies children and to some degree condemns the attitude of most adults. It even explores the idea that children are somehow more spiritually advanced than adults, more capable of seeing with the soul rather than the eyes.

Questions About Innocence

1. In what ways is Seymour innocent? In what ways is he not? What does "innocence" mean in this story, anyway?
2. How is the adult world characterized in this story? The world of children?
3. When do these two worlds come in conflict? What are the consequences?

Chew on Innocence

Seymour is better suited to the world of children than to the world of adults.

Theme of Madness

"A Perfect Day for Bananafish" features a young man who has returned from his service in World War II and is experiencing what today we would call post-traumatic stress disorder. Back in the 1940s, however, this term hadn't even been coined, and people were far less informed about this sort of mental illness. The protagonist, then, is highly misunderstood by the adults around him, so he instead seeks refuge in the world of children, where his "madness" amounts to little more than joking banter. The story makes us wonder what really counts as "insane," even calling into question the "normal" conversations between "sane" adults.

Questions About Madness

1. How does Salinger let us know about Seymour's mental condition without directly spelling it out? What hints does he give us?
2. Does Muriel care about Seymour's mental condition? Does she understand it? Does she take it seriously?
3. What does Seymour's condition have to do with the war?
4. How sympathetic is the world to Seymour's condition? Is this fair?

Chew on Madness

Seymour shoots himself when he realizes that real innocence isn't possible in a corrupt world.

Theme of Spirituality

Salinger wrote "A Perfect Day for Bananafish" when he was highly interested in Zen Buddhism. The epigraph to this story's collection suggests that we approach each tale as though it were a Zen k?an, a riddle with no logical answer. "Bananafish" in many ways rejects logical knowledge in favor of spiritual wisdom. It also condemns materialism as a great danger to the soul's well-being.

Questions About Spirituality

1. What's up with Seymour's nickname for Muriel, "Miss Spiritual Tramp of 1948"?
2. What does Seymour mean when he tells Muriel that he doesn't want people to look at his tattoo?
3. Why does Sybil like Seymour so much? Why does Seymour like Sybil so much?

Chew on Spirituality

Seymour's suicide is tantamount to a spiritual victory.

Theme of Isolation

This story explores the isolating effects of mental illness. Seymour Glass, a troubled young man just back from service in World War II, has difficulty adjusting to being home, no doubt as a result of his experiences in the war. In some ways Seymour self-isolates, but in other ways he is alienated by "normal" society that doesn't understand his mental condition. This isolation is physical, mental, and spiritual – Seymour finds himself "alone" in more ways than one.

Questions About Isolation

1. How close are Seymour and Muriel?
2. Does Seymour form a real connection with Sybil, or does he remain isolated from the rest of the world?
3. Is Seymour fit for society? (Or maybe we should ask if society is fit for Seymour...)

Chew on Isolation

Salinger portrays Seymour as superior to the other materialistic adults in his story.

Theme of Sex

In "A Perfect Day for Bananafish," sex is one of the material pursuits that poses a threat to the well-being of the soul. In the Zen spirit of this work, physical pleasures have no real value and

only distract us from pursuing that which really matters. Most of the story's commentary on sex lies between the lines, or can be inferred from reading some of Salinger's other works on the same characters.

Questions About Sex

1. What can we infer about Seymour and Muriel's sexual relationship? What hints are we given in the text?
2. At first, are we meant to suspect some inappropriate sexual tinge to Seymour and Sybil's friendship? Does this seem intentional on Salinger's part? Once the story is over, does your opinion about this change?
3. How does Seymour feel about sex? You'll find it useful to check out some of Salinger's other stories about Seymour ("Raise High the Roofbeam, Carpenters" is a good start).

Chew on Sex
Seymour kills himself out of shame for his sexual desire for Sybil.

Innocence Quotes
She was a girl who for a ringing phone dropped exactly nothing. She looked as if her phone had been ringing continually ever since she had reached puberty. (1.2)

Thought: Muriel comes across as being one of those popular, beautiful, materialistic girls. There's a shallowness to her character that contrasts with, say, Sybil's pureness.

She washed her comb and brush. She took the spot out of the skirt of her beige suit. She moved the button on her Saks blouse. She tweezed out two freshly surfaced hairs in her mole. When the operator finally rang her room, she was sitting on the window seat and had almost finished putting lacquer on the nails of her left hand. (1.1)

Thought: Materialism is a hallmark of the adult world in this short story.

She went over to the window seat for her cigarettes, lit one, and returned to her seat on the bed. "Mother?" she said, exhaling smoke. (1.44)

Thought: Notice that Muriel is indoors, and surrounded by smoke and nail polish. The atmosphere is very different from that in which Seymour is placed – outside, on the beach, in the sun and the clean air.

"I just got here, Mother. This is the first vacation I've had in years, and I'm not going to just pack everything and come home," said the girl. (1.60)

Thought: Muriel's reasons for staying are essentially selfish; she isn't considering Seymour or his well-being.

"I couldn't travel now anyway. I'm so sunburned I can hardly move." (1.60)

Thought: Some critics think that the sun/sun block/paleness of various characters is a metaphor for different degrees of innocence. See "Symbols, Imagery, Allegory" for more.

"Well. How's your blue coat?"

"All right. I had some of the padding taken out." (1.83-4)

Thought: Many have pointed out the color imagery in "Perfect Day for Bananafish" and suggested that blue represents innocence; check out "Symbols, Imagery, Allegory" for the scoop.

"All right. Just all right, though. We couldn't get the room we had before the war," said the girl. (1.87)

Thought: In other words, things are fundamentally different after the war than they were before.

"He won't take his bathrobe off? Why not?"

"I don't know. I guess because he's so pale." (1.104-5)

Thought: There's that sun imagery again. If getting sun represents being jaded by wordly experiences, then Seymour has taken steps to preserve his innocence.

"See more glass," said Sybil Carpenter, who was staying at the hotel with her mother. "Did you see more glass?"

"Pussycat, stop saying that. It's driving Mommy absolutely crazy. Hold still, please." (2.1-2)

Thought: Notice that a child identifies this key insight about Seymour, while her mother, an adult, misses it completely.

"It was really just an ordinary silk handkerchief – you could see when you got up close," said the woman in the beach chair beside Mrs. Carpenter's. "I wish I knew how she tied it. It was really darling." (4)

Thought: Just like Muriel and her mother, these women appear shallow and materialistic in contrast to Seymour and Sybil.

Sybil stopped walking and yanked her hand away from him. She picked up an ordinary beach shell and looked at it with elaborate interest. She threw it down. (2.48)

Thought: Sybil is characterized by the curiosity and interest typical of young children.

The young man suddenly picked up one of Sybil's wet feet, which were drooping over the end of the float, and kissed the arch. (2.91)

Thought: This small movement demonstrates such reverence and love for youth and innocence on Seymour's part.

"I see you're looking at my feet," he said to her when the car was in motion.

"I beg your pardon?" said the woman.

"I said I see you're looking at my feet."

"I beg your pardon. I happened to be looking at the floor," said the woman, and faced the doors of the car. (2.2-5)

Thought: This is the first time that Seymour seems strange to us. What's so interesting is that his behavior hasn't changed at all since he was joking around with Sybil. While that sort behavior may be perfectly acceptable around children, it appears mad, or crazy, in the adult world.

Madness Quotes

She sat down on one of the made-up twin beds and – it was the fifth or sixth ring – picked up the phone. (1.2)

Thought: It sounds here like Muriel is selfish or at least self-centered. We have to wonder how this affects the way she deals with Seymour's madness.

"Did he try any of that funny business with the trees?" (1.23)

Thought: Salinger very subtly informs his reader of Seymour's madness without giving us too many explicit details.

"He told him everything. At least, he said he did – you know your father. The trees. That business with the window. Those horrible things he said to Granny about her plans for passing away. What he did with all those lovely pictures from Bermuda – everything." (1.49)

Thought: Seymour seems to have a very different take on death than most people. It's likely that whatever he said to "Granny" about her "passing away" was not taken in the spirit it was intended.

"Well. In the first place, he said it was a perfect crime the Army released him from the hospital – my word of honor. He very definitely told your father there's a chance – a very great chance, he said – that Seymour may completely lose control of himself. My word of honor." (1.51)

Thought: Much of the tension of the story is introduced this way; we wonder if, indeed, Seymour will "lose control of himself" by the end of the story.

"You know Seymour," said the girl, and crossed her legs again. "He says he doesn't want a lot of fools looking at his tattoo."

"He doesn't have any tattoo! Did he get one in the Army?"

"No, Mother. No, dear," said the girl, and stood up. (1.107-9)

Thought: Here, we suspect that Muriel actually does understand something about Seymour. It's perfectly clear to her that he's speaking metaphorically, while her mother is left in the dark.

"See more glass," said Sybil Carpenter, who was staying at the hotel with her mother. "Did you see more glass?"

"Pussycat, stop saying that. It's driving Mommy absolutely crazy. Hold still, please." (2.1-2)

Thought: Important spiritual insights are often taken for nonsense or gibberish in this story.

"My daddy's coming tomorrow on a nairiplane," Sybil said, kicking sand.

[…] "Well, it's about time he got here, your daddy. I've been expecting him hourly. Hourly." (2.17-18)

Thought: Seymour's nonsensical conversation has a place with Sybil – this is a perfectly acceptable, playful way to talk to children.

Ask me something else, Sybil," he said. "That's a fine bathing suit you have on. If there's one thing I like, it's a blue bathing suit."

Sybil stared at him, then looked down at her protruding stomach. "This is a yellow," she said. "This is a yellow."

"It is? Come a little closer." Sybil took a step forward. "You're absolutely right. What a fool I am." (20.20-22)

Thought: At this point, we know that Seymour is mentally unstable because of Muriel's conversation with her mother. So all his comments to Sybil leave us guessing: is he really unstable, or just playfully joking with this little girl?

"Yes. Yes, I do," said the young man. "What I like particularly about her is that she never does anything mean to little dogs in the lobby of the hotel. That little toy bull that belongs to that lady from Canada, for instance. You probably won't believe this, but some little girls like to poke that little dog with balloon sticks. Sharon doesn't. She's never mean or unkind. That's why I like her so much."

Sybil was silent. (2.64-5)

Thought: Passages like this one can convince us of Seymour's sanity. He's clearly joking with Sybil, as any adult who is great with children might. He even takes an opportunity to reprimand her – if playfully – as an authoritative adult.

"I see you're looking at my feet," he said to her when the car was in motion.

"I beg your pardon?" said the woman.

"I said I see you're looking at my feet."

"I beg your pardon. I happened to be looking at the floor," said the woman, and faced the doors of the car. (2.2-5)

Thought: This is the first time that Seymour appears to us to be abnormal. What's so interesting is that his behavior hasn't changed at all since he was joking around with Sybil. While this behavior might be perfectly acceptable around children, it appears inappropriate in the adult world.

Spirituality Quotes

"All right, all right. He calls me Miss Spiritual Tramp of 1948," the girl said, and giggled. (1.34)

Thought: This gives us some insight into Muriel's relationship with Seymour. Her giggle implies that she doesn't take him too seriously – which may or may not be a good thing. On the one hand, she misses the gravity of his illness. On the other hand, she balances out his serious, moody spirituality. Check out Salinger's story, "Raise High the Roofbeam, Carpenters," for more insights.

He's played the piano both nights we've been here." (1.70)

Thought: We know from the other Glass stories that Seymour is a poet; now we are reminded again that he is, at heart, a sort of artist.

"I don't know, Mother. I guess because he's so pale and all," said the girl. "Anyway, after Bingo he and his wife asked me if I wouldn't like to join them for a drink. So I did. His wife was horrible. You remember that awful dinner dress we saw in Bonwit's window? The one you said you'd have to have a tiny, tiny – " (1.74)

Thought: Muriel is so distracted by materialistic things like fashion that she can't focus on the matter at hand, what the psychiatrist had to say about Seymour. Spiritually, she is at a very different place than is her husband.

"You know Seymour," said the girl, and crossed her legs again. "He says he doesn't want a lot of fools looking at his tattoo."

"He doesn't have any tattoo! Did he get one in the Army?"

"No, Mother. No, dear," said the girl, and stood up. (1.107-9)

Thought: Much of what Seymour says implies a hidden – and often spiritual – meaning.

"See more glass," said Sybil Carpenter, who was staying at the hotel with her mother. "Did you see more glass?" (2.1)

Thought: Sybil reveals a key insight here: Seymour can *see more* than others.

Mrs. Carpenter was putting sun-tan oil on Sybil's shoulders, spreading it down over the delicate, winglike blades of her back. (2.3)

Thought: Notice that Sybil's shoulder-blades are described as "wing-like." Salinger implies that there is something angelic about her childlike innocence.

"The lady?" the young man brushed some sand out of his thin hair. "That's hard to say, Sybil. She may be in any one of a thousand places. At the hairdresser's. Having her hair dyed mink. Or making dolls for poor children, in her room." (2.20)

Thought: What does this tell us about Seymour's perception of his wife?

"Well, they swim into a hole where there's a lot of bananas. They're very ordinary-looking fish when they swim in. But once they get in, they behave like pigs. Why, I've known some bananafish to swim into a banana hole and eat as many as seventy-eight bananas." He edged the float and its passenger a foot closer to the horizon. "Naturally, after that they're so fat they can't get out of the hole again. Can't fit through the door." (2.35)

Thought: Some critics have claimed that this metaphor refers to the way humans gorge themselves on material pleasures. We'll talk about this more in "What's Up with the Title?"

He got off at the fifth floor, walked down the hall, and let himself into 507. The room smelled of new calfskin luggage and nail-lacquer remover. (2.108)

Thought: This is an entirely different environment than the outdoor setting of the story's first half. There's something artificial and materialistic about the hotel room.

Isolation Quotes

She washed her comb and brush. She took the spot out of the skirt of her beige suit. She moved the button on her Saks blouse. She tweezed out two freshly surfaced hairs in her mole. When the operator finally rang her room, she was sitting on the window seat and had almost finished putting lacquer on the nails of her left hand. (1.1)

Thought: Muriel's materialism sets her markedly apart from Seymour. With such fundamental differences, we wonder how close the two of them are.

"Mother," the girl interrupted, "listen to me. You remember that book he sent me from Germany? You know – those German poems. What'd I do with it? I've been racking my – " (1.36)

Thought: Seymour is clearly quite earnest in asking Muriel to read the poems (Rilke, we can infer). But she doesn't take his request seriously at all, and instead misplaces the book he so valued.

"I mean all he does is lie there. He won't take his bathrobe off." (1.103)

Thought: Seymour makes attempts to insulate and isolate himself from the rest of the world. He's afraid to reveal any of himself.

"The lady?" the young man brushed some sand out of his thin hair. "That's hard to say, Sybil. She may be in any one of a thousand places. At the hairdresser's. Having her hair dyed mink. Or making dolls for poor children, in her room." (2.20)

Thought: This passage reminds us that Seymour and Muriel are never actually together at any point in this story – until Seymour's death at the end.

Lying prone now, he made two fists, set one on top of the other, and rested his chin on the top one. "Ask me something else, Sybil," he said. (2.20)

Thought: Seymour is desperate to make a connection with Sybil. His interactions with her constitute the only real relationship he has in this story.

Sex Quotes

She read an article in a women's pocket-size magazine, called "Sex Is Fun-or Hell." (1.1)

Thought: This theme is introduced to the text early. Salinger gets us thinking (and speculating) about Seymour and Muriel's sexual relationship.

"I said he drove very nicely, Mother. Now, please. I asked him to stay close to the white line, and all, and he knew what I meant, and he did. He was even trying not to look at the trees-you could tell. Did Daddy get the car fixed, incidentally?" (1.24)

Thought: We can infer from this passage that Seymour, perhaps intentionally, drove a car into a tree. Some readers have posited that this aggression is sexual in nature.

"Sybil," he said, "you're looking fine. It's good to see you. Tell me about yourself." He reached in front of him and took both of Sybil's ankles in his hands. "I'm Capricorn," he said. "What are you?" (2.26)

Thought: Do you think that Seymour's conversation with Sybil borders on the flirtatious?

"Sharon Lipschutz said you let her sit on the piano seat with you," Sybil said.

[…]

"Next time, push her off," Sybil said. (2.27-37)

Thought: Sybil definitely has a harmless crush on Seymour.

"I was sitting there, playing. And you were nowhere in sight. And Sharon Lipschutz came over and sat down next to me. I couldn't push her off, could I?"

"Yes."

"Oh, no. No. I couldn't do that," said the young man. "I'll tell you what I did do, though."

"What?"

"I pretended she was you." (2.30-34)

Thought: Seymour's conversation with Sybil alternates between adult flirtation and child-like jokes.

The young man suddenly picked up one of Sybil's wet feet, which were drooping over the end of the float, and kissed the arch. (2.92)

Thought: This is the point in the story where the reader, if he or she has suspected any sexual motivation on Seymour's part, might re-evaluate. This movement seems to reveal reverence, rather than sexual desire.

He glanced at the girl lying asleep on one of the twin beds. Then he went over to one of the pieces of luggage, opened it, and from under a pile of shorts and undershirts he took out an Ortgies calibre 7.65 automatic. He released the magazine, looked at it, then reinserted it. He cocked the piece. Then he went over and sat down on the unoccupied twin bed, looked at the girl, aimed the pistol, and fired a bullet through his right temple. (1.109)

Thought: At this point, the reader either feels bad for suspecting Seymour of pedophilia, or vindicated (if he or she suspects that Seymour killed himself out of guilt for his sexual desires).

Plot Analysis

Classic Plot Analysis

Initial Situation

Muriel, "a girl who for a ringing phone dropped exactly nothing" (1.2).
The very start of "Bananafish" is devoted to Muriel Glass, to what she's like and to who she is. Muriel sets the stage for the story's coming conflict.

Conflict

"Seymour may completely lose control of himself" (1.51).
Muriel's mother's concern for her daughter is the clear conflict here, and it's all about Seymour Glass. We find out that he's got some mental troubles, that they have something to do with the war, and that he's a risk to himself and others (especially given "that business with the trees").

Complication

Is Seymour insane or enlightened?
The scene between Seymour and Sybil certainly complicates the opinion of Seymour we formed during the opening scene. It seems possible that he is in fact the normal one, while everyone else (Mrs. Carpenter, Muriel, her mother) is insane for focusing themselves on things like fashion and drinks at the neglect of their souls. This has a lot to do with the way you interpret 1) the epigraph and 2) the bananafish symbol.

Climax

Seymour kisses Sybil's foot.
This climax is almost as confusing as the story's conclusion. Does Seymour kiss Sybil with affection? Reverence? Sadness? Desire? This climax is definitely tied into the story's title and major themes (see "What's Up with the Title?"), since Sybil has just claimed to have seen a bananafish.

Suspense

Seymour is in an elevator with another adult.
Seymour has finally left the world of children and for the first time in the story is thrown into contact with another adult. That this takes place in an elevator is rather ingenious – it raises the stakes on the tension. (They're trapped together; there's nowhere for either of them to go.) The reader should at this moment remember everything Muriel's mother said at the start of the text: that Seymour is unstable and might completely lose control of himself.

Denouement

Seymour kills himself.
Unlike most denouements, little is resolved or explained during this falling action. The suspense is resolved in the sense that we no longer wonder what Seymour is going to do, but we also aren't left with any satisfying explanation for his mental illness.

Conclusion

Ambiguous
As we discuss in "What's Up with the Ending?", the ending to "Bananafish" is highly enigmatic. The story has no clear conclusion or, rather, the conclusion is a question (perhaps a k?an, if you've read "What's Up With the Epigraph?"): why does Seymour commit suicide?

Study Questions

1. How does the Seymour of Salinger's other Glass family stories differ from the Seymour of "Perfect Day for Bananafish"?
2. In what ways is Seymour similar to Holden Caulfield, the protagonist of Salinger's novel *Catcher in the Rye*? Why do these two characters, similar in many ways, end up in such different places?
3. There are a number of references to other writers and literary works in "A Perfect Day for Bananafish" (see "Shout Outs" for a full list). How do these other works or authors inform and comment on this story?
4. How would the second half of the story be read, had we not first witnessed the conversation between Muriel and her mother? How does this first scene inform the second one?
5. Consider the use of numbers in "A Perfect Day for Bananafish." (Room 507, six bananas, six tigers, the 7.65 automatic.) Is there anything going on here?
6. The Big Question: Why does Seymour kill himself? Is there supposed to be a clear answer to this question, or not?

Characters

All Characters

Seymour Glass Character Analysis

Before we meet Seymour, we hear that there's something wrong with him. Salinger uses Muriel's conversation with her mother to preface Seymour's interaction with Sybil. We have to do a pretty careful job of reading between the lines here to figure out what's up; very little is explicit or obvious, so we infer and deduce the scenario by looking at little hints.

Muriel's mom asks over and over again if Muriel is safe and if Seymour is behaving himself. Her references to Seymour's behavior in the past – funny business with trees, inappropriate comments about death, something to do with a window – all suggest that Seymour is emotionally unstable. We even gather that he intentionally drove a car into a tree. When Muriel's mother mentions a Dr. Sivetski, we know that they've gotten Seymour into psychotherapy. And then comes the big warning: "There's a chance – a very great chance, he said – that Seymour may completely lose control of himself" (51).

This should worry us a little bit, or at least raise our concern for Seymour. But Muriel is so

cavalier about her husband's condition that our fears are somewhat put to rest. Perhaps this is just a case of an overanxious, overprotective mother who doesn't really like her son-in-law?

Then again, perhaps not. We do get a bit more information before we head on to scene number two. We find out that Seymour has only recently come back from the war (World War II, as this is 1948), and that he spent some time in army hospital – presumably for whatever mental or emotional troubles he's still experiencing now – before coming home. Now we're thinking along the lines of PTSD, or post-traumatic stress disorder. Today, the world is well-informed about this condition, and most people are sensitive to it. But in the 1940s, when Salinger was writing, PTSD wasn't really a buzz-word yet. (The phrase wasn't even coined until the 1970s.) So instead of trying to help or understand Seymour, most people are reacting to him in the same way as Muriel's mother. They think he's weird, and they'd rather just avoid him at all costs.

And so the stage is set, all before we meet our main character. What happens when we actually do encounter Seymour? Let's consider his interaction with Sybil. For starters, he's funny. He's engaging, entertaining, kind, and obviously amazing with children. He plays with Sybil and even tries to teach her a lesson or two (as when he gently reprimands her for teasing the dogs in the hotel lobby).

But there's more to this scene. For starters, Seymour is alone on a deserted part of the beach. He's isolated himself from other adults and comes off as something of a loner. Before Sybil comes along, he's lying down in a tightly cinched-up bathrobe, which strikes us as a bit odd for a tourist on a beach in Florida.

Then, of course, we have to consider the nature of his interaction with Sybil. Jaded and cynical readers will want to know why a grown man has chosen to cultivate a friendship with a four-year-old girl while snubbing adult society. They might even suspect that there's a shade of pedophilia in his relationship with her. (Critics are definitely divided on this topic. See "Sex" for a full discussion of the ambiguity.) What we do know is that Sybil's relationship with Seymour is hugely important to this story – which we'll discuss in Sybil's "Character Analysis." We also know that their conversation is potentially loaded with hidden meaning, metaphor, and symbols, which we explore in "Symbols, Imagery, Allegory."

Back to Seymour. After the scene with Sybil, we're still not really sure about his mental health. Maybe he is mentally unstable, or maybe he's just a loner who happens to love children and has been completely misinterpreted by more materialistic people like Muriel's mom.

But we're done guessing after the elevator scene. Seymour, for no apparent reason, accuses a woman of staring at his feet, calling her a "god-damned sneak" (104). He then goes into his room and kills himself. Now we know for sure – Seymour is unstable.

Which brings us to the big question: why does Seymour kill himself? There is no one answer to this question, but we discuss many different options in "What's Up with the Ending?" It's also possible that there is no answer, which we discuss in "What's Up with the Epigraph."

Seymour Glass Timeline and Summary

- We find out from Muriel's conversation with her mother that Seymour recently got out of the army and has some sort of mental illness. While Muriel's mother is greatly concerned, Muriel is not.
- Cut to Seymour on the beach, lying in his bathrobe. Sybil and he make conversation; it's clear that they've become friends while staying at the hotel.
- Seymour and Sybil banter for a bit; Seymour jokes with her about the color of her bathing suit and Sharon Lipschutz.
- Finally Seymour decides to go into the water. He takes off his bathrobe to reveal his blue swim trunks. He folds the towel neatly and takes Sybil's hand to walk into the water.
- Seymour tells Sybil about the bananafish.
- In the ocean, Seymour puts Sybil on the raft and lets her get a little soaked from the waves.
- When Sybil claims that she's seen a bananafish, Seymour kisses the arch of her foot and then tells her they're going in.
- Back on the beach, Sybil says good-bye and leaves. Seymour goes back to the hotel, taking the poorly-inflated raft with him.
- In the elevator, Seymour gets angry at a woman for looking at his feet.
- In his hotel room, Seymour shoots himself while Muriel lays sleeping.

Sybil Carpenter Character Analysis

Sybil is a young girl vacationing on Florida with her mother. We can guess that her age is somewhere around four. Salinger tells us she's wearing a two-piece bathing suit, "one piece of which she would not actually be needing for another nine or ten years" (3). Later, when she pretends to not know her home town, Seymour tells her that Sharon Lipschutz knows where she lives, "and she's only three and a half" (43).

Sybil is completely characterized by her youth. She examines a seashell "with elaborate interest" before throwing it down (48). She hops on one foot for fun. She likes to eat wax. She walks "stomach foremost" in the manner of small children (48).

Sybil also reveals a number of singular qualities we wouldn't expect from a child. Her name indicated she's a prophet of sorts (check out "Character Clues"), and the description of her shoulder-blades as "wing-like" suggests a unique spiritual quality (which explains some of Seymour's attraction to her). Notice also that Sybil, though maybe without knowing it, uncovers an important insight: Seymour's name sounds the same as "see more." (Again, check out "Character Clues.")

We see in this story the glorification, perhaps even the deification, of youth. One of the central themes of "Bananafish" is the contrast between the world of adults (characterized by Muriel, her mother, and Sybil's mother) and the world of children (exemplified by Sybil). While the former is

shallow, self-involved, selfish, and cynical, the latter is pure, engaging, and even beautiful.

Seymour, though an adult himself, has fled from other grown-ups and taken refuge in the world of children. He's left "the part of the beach reserved for guests of the hotel" (2.8) and has forsaken the company of his wife for solitude and Sybil. "I was waiting for you," he tells Sybil when she shows up (14). And, as we discuss in Seymour's "Character Analysis," he is indeed very much at home in the world of children. He's a genius with Sybil, and she's obviously completely enamored with him (as evidenced by her jealousy over his friendship with Sharon Lipschutz).

Let's look a little more closely at Seymour's relationship with Sybil, in particular at the somewhat confusing and rather abrupt end to their play-date:

With her hand, when the float was level again, she wiped away a flat, wet band of hair from her eyes, and reported, "I just saw one."

"Saw what, my love?"

"A bananafish."

"My God, no!" said the young man. "Did he have any bananas in his mouth?"

"Yes," said Sybil. "Six."

The young man suddenly picked up one of Sybil's wet feet, which were drooping over the end of the float, and kissed the arch.

"Hey!" said the owner of the foot, turning around.

"Hey, yourself. We're going in now. You had enough?"

"No!"

"Sorry," he said, and pushed the float toward shore until Sybil got off it. He carried it the rest of the way.

"Goodbye," said Sybil, and ran without regret in the direction of the hotel. (86-97)

What just happened? They are playing in the waves, joking around, everything is fine, and then suddenly Seymour decides to leave (and possibly decides, at this moment, to kill himself). What's going on?

As usual, we want to look as closely as possible at the text. Seymour is obviously incredibly affected by Sybil's declaration that she has seen a bananafish with six bananas in its mouth. It is this line that prompts him to pick up her foot and kiss it, an action that seems filled with *reverence* for the young girl. One interpretation is that Seymour is filled with love; this little girl is so innocent, her mind so flexible, that she is able to enter into his world of fantasy (which no

adults are able to do). When she shouts "Hey!" afterwards, he's reminded that he's not *allowed* to do things like that (it's not "appropriate" in the real world), and he ends their time together.

Another possibility is that he's kissing Sybil good-bye. When she yells that she's seen a bananafish, Seymour thinks she's talking about him (in other words, that Seymour himself is the bananafish. Check out more on this theory in "What's Up with the Title?"). Consumed with guilt, he decides then and there to kill himself and so is saying good-bye.

Another (less popular) possibility is that Seymour is sexually attracted to Sybil and kisses her out of desire. When she shouts "Hey!" he's filled with shame and decides to kill himself.

What we see next is certainly telling. Seymour plods along back to the hotel and gets into an elevator with an adult woman. "I see you're looking at my feet," he says (102). This is exactly the sort of silly banter Seymour was engaged in with Sybil only a few minutes earlier. But now, he is met with hostility and accusation instead of adoration. "I happened to be looking at the floor," responds the woman (105). Seymour, while perfectly suited to the world of children, is entirely incapable of functioning in the world of adults. What's interesting is that the tone of "Bananafish" may suggest that this is the adults' problem – not Seymour's.

Sybil Carpenter Timeline and Summary

- Sybil repeats "see more glass" while her mother puts suntan oil on her shoulders. When her mother tells her to run off and play, she heads down the beach to find Seymour.
- Sybil wants to go in the water with Seymour. She tells him that her father is coming soon, and notes that his float needs air.
- Sybil reveals that she's jealous over Seymour's paying attention to Sharon Lipschutz.
- As she and Seymour head into the water, Sybil and Seymour discuss *Little Black Sambo*.
- In the ocean, Sybil rides on the float. Sybil listens while he describes bananafish.
- Sybil tells Seymour not to let her get wet, but enjoys it anyway when she gets soaked by a wave.
- Sybil exclaims that she's seen a bananafish with six bananas in its mouth.
- She yells when Seymour kisses the arch of her foot and protests when he says they're going back to shore.
- Back on the beach, Sybil says good-bye and runs "without regret" in the direction of the hotel.

Muriel Glass Character Analysis

Muriel is Seymour's young wife. At first, it might be difficult to see why a man like Seymour is married to a woman like Muriel. He's spiritual and introspective; she's materialistic and social. He takes everything seriously; she's light as a feather. Everything Muriel does and says seems

shallow, even more so after we watch Seymour interact with Sybil and then commit suicide. Their marriage sounds like a total mismatch.

If you really want to get a handle on this relationship, you might take a look at some of Salinger's other stories revolving around Seymour and the rest of the Glass family. "Raise High the Roofbeam, Carpenters" is a narration of Seymour and Muriel's wedding; or rather, the lack of wedding (the two elope last minute, to the dismay of Muriel's family). It features one of Seymour's diary entries and goes some way in explaining his feelings for Muriel. In a shamelessly simplified summation, she balances him out. She's sort of like his connection to the rest of the world.

Given Seymour's spirituality and wisdom, we can be pretty sure that he "gets" Muriel. But how well does Muriel understand her husband? Readers are continually struck by Muriel's cavalier indifference in the story's first few pages. Therapists think her husband is unstable. He's deliberately driven a car into a tree; he's obviously suffering mentally from his experiences in the war, and she's gabbing about fashion and giggling about his nickname for her. As it's unlikely that Muriel doesn't care about her husband, we can only conclude that she doesn't get it. She doesn't recognize the severity of the situation.

One of the enigmas of the story's ending is why Seymour chooses to kill himself in the presence of his wife, and why he doesn't wake her up before he does it. The image of the final scene is a lasting one; Muriel sleeps on one twin bed while Seymour fires a bullet through his temple. This so perfectly encapsulates the degree to which Muriel is unaware of her husband's plight. If you're interested in spirituality and Buddhism as a theme of "Bananafish," you can think about Muriel's spiritual status as compared to Seymour's. Because she's so caught up in materialistic needs, she's "asleep" and is missing what is more important.

Muriel Glass Timeline and Summary

- While waiting for a phone line to open up, Muriel reads a magazine article, moves a button on her blouse, and paints her nails.
- While on the phone with her mother, Muriel repeats over and over that she's fine. It soon becomes clear that her husband, Seymour, has some sort of mental illness. While this concerns her mother, it doesn't seem to worry Muriel too much.
- Muriel giggles over Seymour's nickname for her, "Miss Spiritual Tramp of 1948."
- She asks her mother if she left the book of German poems Seymour gave her at home, as she can't find it.
- They discuss Dr. Sivetski and his opinion of Seymour. We find out that Muriel waited for Seymour while he was in the army during the war.
- Muriel tells her mother that there is a therapist staying at the hotel, though she hasn't had time to talk with him seriously about Seymour.
- The two women move on to chatting about clothes and fashion. Muriel's mother makes one last plea for Muriel to come home before hanging up. Muriel insists everything is fine.

Character Roles

Protagonist

Seymour Glass

Seymour is the focus and central enigma of "A Perfect Day for Bananafish." Though he's not present for the first half of the story, Muriel's conversation with her mother still resolves around Seymour, and it is with his story that we are primarily concerned.

Antagonist

Materialism

This brings us back to the story's spiritual theme, discussed in "What's Up with the Epigraph." Seymour fights against the material concerns that consume the other adult sin the story; he avoids falling into the habits of the bananafish who contract banana fever after gorging themselves on a disgusting amount of bananas.

Foil

Children and Adults

The contrast between the world occupied by Sybil and Seymour and that of the adults in the story (Mrs. Carpenter, Muriel, and Muriel's mother) is rather blunt. These women are obsessed with frivolous matters like fashion or appearances or food or drink; Sybil and Seymour are unbothered by these materialistic trivialities.

Character Clues

Names

As Sybil so adorably points out, Seymour Glass sounds a lot like "see more glass." Seymour sees more, presumably, than the rest of us can see. As we discuss in "What's Up with the Ending?", spirituality and Zen Buddhism were important concepts for Salinger. That he gives Seymour this special spiritual distinction is not surprising.

Speaking of Sybil, consider "Sybil Carpenter" as a name. In Ancient Greece, "sybils" were prophetesses, or female seers. They could predict the future. In this way, Sybil, too, sees more. She and Seymour are distinct from the story's other characters in that they are both spiritually advanced (especially in comparison to the materialistic adult women). Think also about the description of Sybil's shoulder blades as "winglike" (2.3)– this is no ordinary four-year-old. The last name "Carpenter" is also striking, as it brings to mind Jesus Christ, who was…a carpenter. We'll let you decide what to do with that.

Speech and Dialogue

"A Perfect Day for Bananafish" contains almost no exposition (straight-up telling) whatsoever. And yet we walk away from this story with a very good sense of its main characters (Seymour, Muriel, Sybil, even Mrs. Carpenter). That's because of Salinger's extraordinary dialogue –

which takes up about 90% of the text.

Consider Muriel's conversation with her mother. We know that Muriel is materialistic, her mother protective, Seymour unstable, their marriage precarious and eccentric – all without any direct telling. The complexities in Seymour's dialogue with Sybil are similarly implicit. A single line of dialogue holds any number of important meanings (check out "Symbols, Imagery, Allegory" for a trove of examples).

Literary Devices

Symbols, Imagery, Allegory

A Note Before We Start

Before we talk about any of these symbols, you should know that there are two camps when it comes to interpreting "A Perfect Day for Bananafish." One camp is all about the deep hidden meaning, thinking that every line, perhaps even every word has some carefully chosen significance. From this viewpoint, it matters that Seymour's room is 507, rather than 213. It matters that Seymour's swim trunks are blue. It matters that Sybil likes to eat wax, not jellybeans or pencils. The other camp bases its interpretation largely on the epigraph, which tells us not to approach this story with logic. To pick it apart analytically is to misinterpret Salinger's intentions.

We're going to go ahead and discuss the possible meanings of these different symbols, but keep in mind that it might all be for naught.

The Bananafish

We discuss this central theme in "What's Up with the Title?" See you there.

The Color Blue

Notice that Seymour's swim trunks are blue, while Sybil wears a yellow bathing suit. Yet Seymour says to her, "That's a fine bathing suit you have on. If there's one thing I like, it's a blue bathing suit" (2.20). If we think of blue as associated with purity or innocence, then it makes sense that Seymour is wearing blue trunks. It also makes sense that he thinks Sybil is wearing a blue bathing suit. She is pure and innocent, so he associates her with the color blue.

Actually, there's an interesting aside in Salinger's short story "Raise High the Roofbeam, Carpenters" that Buddy Glass tells about his brother Seymour. When their sister Franny was a ten months old, Seymour read her a story to stop her from fussing one night. The story he read was a Taoist tale about Duke Mu of China and an enlightened man named Po Lo. The Duke asked Po Lo to send him a man who could pick out a superior horse from a group of animals. Po Lo does, and the Duke employs this man to pick out a horse for him. The man does, and when the emperor asks about its color and sex, the man tells him it is a brown mare. When the horse arrives, however, it is a black stallion. The Duke is peeved that this guy can't even tell the color and sex of a horse, but Po Lo is ecstatic. The man has learned to look at the horse's

"spiritual mechanism," he says. "In making sure of the essential, he forgets the homely details; intent on the inward qualities, he loses sight of the external."

That's seems to be what's going on here with Seymour. Seymour sees Sybil's spiritual mechanism, her internal qualities of purity and innocence. So he sees her in the color blue, rather than the yellow she actually wears.

Sunburns

Notice that Seymour is very pale and doesn't want to get any sun on the beach. Muriel, on the other hand, is inside because she's sun-burned so badly. Getting too much sun is sort of equivalent to getting burned by material pursuits. Or, it could be equivalent to being jaded by experiences in the world. If this is the case, Seymour has maintained his spiritual purity or his youthful innocence, while Muriel has not. You might also want to consider the woman in the elevator with zinc salve on her nose, or the fact that Sybil is being slathered with sun-tan oil when we first meet her.

Setting

A resort hotel in Florida, 1948

We know from Seymour's nickname for Muriel that the year is 1948. In later Glass family works, narrator Buddy Glass confirms that his brother Seymour committed suicide in 1948, allowing us to deduce that Seymour was 30 or 31 at the time.

It's interesting to consider the sort of dual setting we have in this story. The first half takes place in a hotel room indoors, where a sun-burnt Muriel talks on the phone to her mother. The second half takes place outside, in the sun and in the ocean, where a pale Seymour plays with young Sybil. It's appropriate that Muriel is indoors; she's materialistic and certainly less aware of the world (at least spiritually) than Seymour. It's also appropriate that Sybil and Seymour are outside, in the purity of the natural elements. It's striking that when Seymour enters the hotel room, he is immediately hit with the smell of "new calfskin luggage and nail-lacquer remover" (2.108). This world – the materialistic world of his wife – is very different than the pure, natural world he just occupied with Sybil.

Narrator Point of View

Third Person (Omniscient); but also First Person (Peripheral Narrator)

If you look only at the text of "Bananafish," you see an omniscient third person narrator. It might as well be a fly on the wall telling the story – the narrator doesn't know anything about these characters other than what he sees. Notice that the narrator never tells us that Seymour just came back from the war; instead, he observes Muriel and her mother discussing the fact that Seymour just came back from the war. Similarly, Muriel is referred to as "the young woman" and Seymour as "the young man" in narration.

But, check out more of Salinger's work on the Glass family, and you'll meet Buddy Glass, Seymour's younger brother and a writer. He claims to be the "hidden" narrator of many (or maybe all) of the Glass stories. At one point there's even the suggestion that Buddy, though trying to describe Seymour's death, unintentionally ends up describing himself in the character named "Seymour." There's plenty more narrative trickiness where that came from: check out *Franny and Zooey* if you find this sort of thing as interesting as we do.

Genre

Literary Fiction

"A Perfect Day for Bananafish" isn't interested in plot or suspense as much as in character and theme. Salinger's narrative technique, dialogue, and powers of characterization have been praised by many critics, as has the structure and effect of "Bananafish" in particular. The psychological complexity of Seymour Glass and the story's enigmatic conclusion have given it solid standing in the short story canon.

Tone

Critical, Aloof

Muriel and the three other adult women in the story are painted in a most unflattering light, bordering on a caricature (*all* they talk about is fashion, even while dismissing the importance of Seymour's mental illness). Their world, priorities, and actions are judged and condemned as materialistic and shallow. As far as Seymour's death is concerned, the authorial tone maintains its distance from the topic at hand, betraying no real opinion of its own on the matter. The author leaves it up to his reader to interpret this tale.

Writing Style

Salinger-esque

Salinger is so famous for his tell-tale writing style, we figured we would just call it what it is. Observe all of these typical Salinger trademarks:

- Italicized words for emphasis give the dialogue a natural phonetic feel.
- Incomplete sentences reflect the way people really talk.
- Physical movements are described in poignant, conscientious detail.
- The narrator is removed from the action but intimately aware of what's important.

In short, you should be able to recognize this as trademark-Salinger even in a dark alley on a windless night.

What's Up with the Title?

The bananafish are one of the story's key symbols. To understand what's going on here, we've got to take a closer look at the text:

"This is a perfect day for bananafish. [...] Their habits are very peculiar. [...] They lead a very tragic life. [...] You know what they do, Sybil? [...] Well, they swim into a hole where there's a lot of bananas. They're very ordinary-looking fish when they swim in. But once they get in, they behave like pigs. Why, I've known some bananafish to swim into a banana hole and eat as many as seventy-eight bananas. [...] Naturally, after that they're so fat they can't get out of the hole again. Can't fit through the door."

[...] "What happens to them?"

[...]

"Oh, you mean after they eat so many bananas they can't get out of the banana hole? [...] Well, I hate to tell you, Sybil. They die. [...] They get banana fever. It's a terrible disease." (2.71-83)

As with most of "Bananafish," there's no one answer or clear interpretation here. One angle you might take is to think about the story's spiritual or Zen Buddhism theme. (See "What's Up with the Epigraph?" for an introduction to this theme.) By stuffing themselves full of bananas, the bananafish are focusing physical needs or pleasures. This is not unlike the materialistic adults in the story (such as Muriel, Muriel's mother, and Mrs. Carpenter) with their talk of clothes, fashion, or drinks. Seymour, who sees more, is aware of this sort of gluttony and wants to avoid it all costs. He doesn't want to gorge himself on bananas.

Which leads us nicely into the discussion of "What's Up with the Ending?" If Seymour is enlightened, then killing himself is a way of triumphing over any material impulses. If Seymour is filled with shame at his death, it may be that he suspects himself of such "banana-fever." (Maybe when Sybil exclaims that she's seen a bananafish, Seymour thinks he's talking about him.) Go ahead and check out "What's Up with the Ending?" for more thoughts.

What's Up with the Epigraph?

We know the sound of two hands clapping. But what is the sound of one hand clapping?
– A Zen K?an

This is the epigraph to *Nine Stories*, the 1953 collection that opens with "A Perfect Day for Bananafish." Together, these nine stories explore themes of innocence, youth, the psychological effects of war, and Zen Buddhism. While Zen isn't explicitly discussed in "Bananafish," it's easy to see this spiritual theme reflected in the story. If this stuff interests you, we'd recommend reading "Bananafish" and "Teddy" (the final piece in the *Nine Stories* collection) together. These two works book-end *Nine Stories*, literally and thematically, and "Teddy" really informs the way that we read and interpret "Bananafish."

In "Teddy," for example, the titular character, an enlightened young man and spiritual prodigy,

explains to a college student the way that knowledge works. His theory is that we are all so distracted and filled up with the useless things we learn in school – like math and science and grammar and logic – that we don't open ourselves to real spiritual truths. To get at those, you have to "empty yourself" of all logical truths. Similarly, in Salinger's novel _Franny and Zooey_, college student Franny Glass (Seymour's younger sister) complains that in school, they learn nothing but this useless knowledge. Their goal is to amass as much of it as quickly as possible, which Franny finds no more noble than trying to amass wealth, fame, or any material good. Knowledge is pointless, she says, unless it ultimately leads to _wisdom_.

Which brings us to the epigraph. A k?an is a sort of riddle, as you can see from this particular example. But the answer to the riddle isn't logical. If we ask you, "What is the square root of 435?" you can solve the problem using the usual parts of your brain (or a handy calculator). The question has logical answer. But k?ans don't work that way. What is the sound of one hand clapping? If you meditate on this long enough, claim the Zen Buddhists, you will come up with an answer. But it's not a logical answer that you could explain to someone else. In other words, you can't Google the answer to this one. You have to intuit it on your own.

What does this have to do with "A Perfect Day for Bananafish"? Remember that the point of an epigraph is to inform the way we read a work. The epigraph provides the author with an opportunity to give us a hint (or sometimes tell us directly) how to interpret his writing. This epigraph reminds us that some questions – actually, the most important questions, spiritually speaking – don't have logical answers. And, of course, the big question in "Bananafish" is…why does Seymour kill himself? It's very possible that Salinger intends his story as a sort of k?an in itself. There may be an answer to his question, but it's not one that anyone could write down or explain in a thesis paper. We're meant to meditate on this and the other stories in the collection, but we're not meant to "figure out" what the "answer" is.

If you buy into this theory, you might very well take issue with all the "deep hidden meaning" conclusions that critics have drawn and that we've explored in "Symbols, Imagery, Allegory." You might think that it's the wrong approach to assign any one meaning to each of the metaphors and images in this text (like the bananafish, the color blue, the nail polish). And this is certainly a legitimate approach to the text. Maybe it's better to walk away from "A Perfect Day for Bananafish" with an emotional or spiritual reaction, rather than an analytical one.

What's Up with the Ending?

Why does Seymour commit suicide? This is possibly one of the most highly-debated short story questions of the last fifty years. There are dozens of theories, and we can't be sure which one of them is "right." It could be that Salinger wrote his story with some specific reason in mind; or it could be that he intentionally left it ambiguous. It also might be, as we argue in "What's Up with the Epigraph," that the "answer" to this question can't be logically conceptualized. In any case, here's a little pupu platter of Seymour theories:

#1) Innocence, Children, and the War
Let's not forget that Seymour's mental troubles are the result of the war, and that he's suffering from what today we would probably call post-traumatic stress disorder (though this

term wasn't yet around when Salinger was writing). We infer that Seymour has witnessed some awful things during his time in the service, and that he's having a hard time readjusting to being home. We see that he's retreated into a largely insular world, and that he's no longer comfortable interacting with most adults. Sybil offers him a glimpse of the world as he would like it to be – innocent, curious, and pure – but his interaction with the woman in the elevator reminds him that the adult world is actually nothing like this. Unable to cope with reality, and unable to function normally, Seymour turns to suicide.

#2) Seymour Is Enlightened

This theory makes more sense if you've read some of Salinger's other works about Seymour, or in particular if you're looking at "Bananafish" as part of the collection *Nine Stories*. As hinted at in the epigraph to *Nine Stories*, there is a common theme of Zen Buddhism in Salinger's work. "Bananafish," the first story of the collection, and "Teddy," the final story, both deal with this theme, though the latter far more explicitly. In "Teddy," a young child genius is somewhat of a Zen master. He discusses his flirtation with enlightenment in a previous life, and he casually foretells his own death.

It's interesting to note that both "Bananafish" and "Teddy" end with the death of the main character. At first, the tone of these deaths may seem very different. Teddy calmly accepts his accidental death as a step on the road to enlightenment, and there is tranquility even in the jarring ending. What of the conclusion to Bananafish, though? Is it a jarring, painful ending, quite different from that of Teddy? Or is Seymour's death, too, a calm and accepting step in the right spiritual direction? In "Teddy," for example, the title character explains that death is in many ways like waking up. It's no coincidence that Muriel is sleeping in the bed nearby when Seymour puts the gun to his head. He's waking up; she's still asleep.

Consider the idea of the bananafish. We flesh out this idea a but more in "What's Up with the Title?" The short version, though, is that the gluttonous bananafish may represent the material obsessions of people. Seymour doesn't want to be like the bananafish, pigging out on physical desires, so he kills himself. He ends his physical existence, but not, many argue, his spiritual one.

#3) Seymour is Sexually Attracted to Sybil

One possible, if far less satisfying, reason for Seymour's suicide is pedophilia. He's attracted to Sybil and even goes so far as to kiss her foot. He's then filled with shame at his action and so kills himself, preserving Sybil's purity in the process. It's unlikely that Salinger intended this as a line of reasoning, but there you have it.

Trivia

- Salinger's story was originally titled "A Fine Day for Bananafish." (Source: Alexander, Paul (1999). *Salinger: A Biography*.)

Steaminess Rating

PG-13

After finishing "Bananafish," you're probably so consumed with sympathy for Seymour that you don't want to admit you ever suspected the poor guy of any sexual interest in Sybil. But your first time through the story, you probably started to feel a little uncomfortable right about here:

"Sybil," he said, "I'll tell you what we'll do. We'll see if we can catch a bananafish."

"A what?"

"A bananafish," he said, and undid the belt of his robe. (2.39-41)

Did Salinger intend this to sound, in a word, sketchy? Or are we just a bunch of cynics who wouldn't know a beautiful and innocent friendship if it smacked us on the nose? Hard to say.

What you want to think about here are the implications for our reading of "Bananafish," particularly Seymour's death. How does the interpretation of this particular moment change the way we interpret the ending? Check out Seymour's "Character Analysis" for more.

Allusions and Cultural References

Literature and Philosophy

- Rainer Maria Rilke (1.36-42) – This is an implicit reference; Rilke is never mentioned by name, only referred to as a German and "the only great poet of the century."
- Helen Bannerman, *Little Black Sambo* (2.52-57)
- T. S. Eliot, "The Wasteland" (2.39) – "…mixing memory and desire…" Seymour takes this quote from the first few lines of Eliot's poem.

Best of the Web

Videos
This will only take thirty seconds.
http://www.youtube.com/watch?v=__9cQ92VZHA

This is actually an extremely well-done short. The music nails the mood of Salinger's story. And the decision to make Sybil imaginary, while not true to the text, is an interesting take. Kudos.

Audios
Salinger Inspires Music
http://www.mp3.com/albums/20132680/summary.html
The Fire Apes' album, *A Perfect Day for Bananafish*

Images
Salinger
http://www.terebess.hu/english/img/salinger2.jpg
Before he became a recluse.

Hardy-Har-Har
http://www.worth1000.com/entries/164500/164982TyBX_w.jpg
This is what happens when you take metaphors literally.

Documents
Online Text
http://www.freeweb.hu/tchl/salinger/perfectday.html
Free!

New York Times Review from 1953
http://www.nytimes.com/books/98/09/13/specials/salinger-stories02.html?scp=3&sq=%22a%20perfect%20day%20for%20bananafish%22&st=cse
"Small monsters and large shadows of the macabre" indeed.

Websites
All those Glass stories can get confusing.
http://www.salinger.org/index.php?title=Glass_family
Clear it up.

Glass Family Quiz
http://www.triv.net/html/Users4/u11251.htm
Test your knowledge.

Printed in Great Britain
by Amazon

64745173R00023